truly me™ School Spirit

Discover your student style with quizzes, activities, crafts—and more!

by Carrie Anton

illustrated by Marilena Perilli,
Hannah Davies,
and Flavia Conley

Published by American Girl Publishing
Copyright © 2015 American Girl

Questions or comments? Call 1-800-845-0005,
visit **americangirl.com**, or write to Customer Service,
American Girl, 8400 Fairway Place, Middleton, WI 53562-0497.

Printed in China
15 16 17 18 19 20 21 LEO 10 9 8 7 6 5 4 3 2 1

All American Girl marks and Truly Me™ are trademarks of American Girl.

Editorial Development: Melissa Seymour, Trula Magruder
Art Direction and Design: Sarah Boecher, Jessica Rogers
Production: Jeannette Bailey, Judith Lary, Paula Moon, Kendra Schluter
Photography: Radlund Photography, Youa Thao
Craft Stylist: Carrie Anton
Wardrobe Stylist: Aubre Andrus
Hair Stylist: Ashley Franklin
Doll Stylist: Meghan Hurley
Illustrations: Marilena Perilli, Hannah Davies, Flavia Conley

Dear Reader,

What does school mean to you? Is it just a place where you sit in class, listen to your teacher, and leave with homework at the end of the day? Or do you see it as something so much more? Is it the place where you meet new people and hang out with old friends? Is it where you discover things you never knew and get excited to find out more? Is it a place you feel connected to, one that will help you reach your dreams?

Whatever school means to you, it's a big part of your life. We've filled the pages of this book with activities, crafts, and quizzes that celebrate you as a student. Next time you wonder about the world, dream about your future, set goals you want to achieve, or just need the support of others, know that you can count on your classmates, teachers, and school to help you along the way.

Gather your creativity, curiosity, and imagination: Class is now in session!

Your friends at American Girl

When you see this symbol ✋, it means you need an adult to help you with all or part of the task. ALWAYS ask for help before continuing. Ask an adult to approve all craft supplies before you use them—some are not safe for kids. When creating doll crafts, remember that dyes from supplies may bleed onto your doll or her clothes and leave permanent stains. Use lighter colors when possible, and check your doll often to make sure the colors aren't transferring to her body, her vinyl, or her clothes. And never get your doll wet! Water and heat increase dye rub-off.

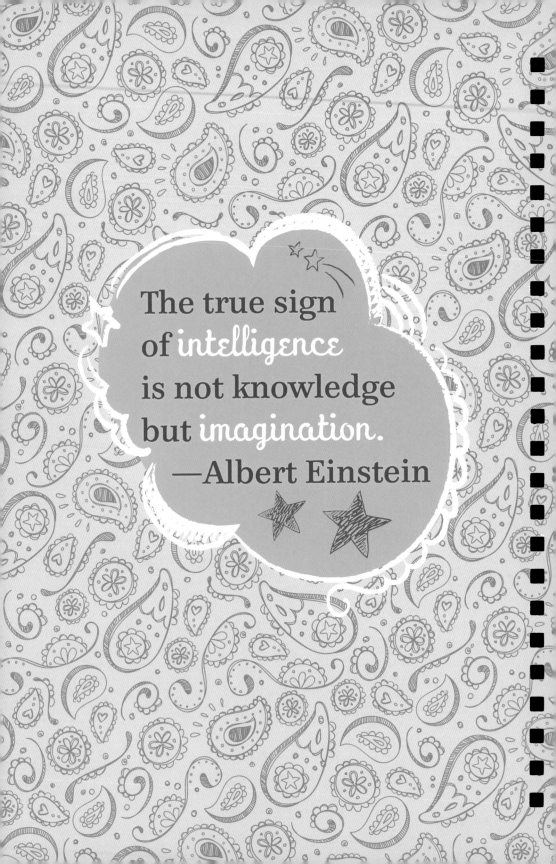

The true sign of *intelligence* is not knowledge but *imagination.*
—Albert Einstein

Star Student

No matter what your interests are, there are special ways for you to shine as a student. Answer the following questions to help discover your very own student style.

1. On a Saturday morning, you feel happiest when you're . . .
   a. reading a book.
   b. playing soccer.
   c. helping your mom with your little sister.
   d. planning a new club with a friend.
   e. singing in the shower.
   f. climbing a tree in the backyard.

2. Your school is putting on a musical, and you want to be involved. You . . .
   a. write and edit the script.
   b. set up the stage and move props.
   c. volunteer wherever you're needed.
   d. spread the word about opening night.
   e. star in the show.
   f. work on sound and lighting.

3. Your friend is bored and asks if you need any help. You ask her to . . .

a. quiz you on multiplication for your math test.

b. play catch since softball season is starting soon.

c. walk the neighbors' dogs with you.

d. make donation signs for the upcoming winter coat drive.

e. read lines to help you practice for the school play.

f. help you plant seeds for your indoor herb garden.

4. Your school needs ideas to help raise money for new gym bleachers. You suggest . . .

a. a community spelling bee for adults and kids to enter.

b. a community 5K run/walk.

c. a class car wash.

d. a candy-bar fund-raiser.

e. a school-hosted movie night.

f. an Earth Day–themed school dance.

5. Your dream birthday present would be . . .

a. your very own laptop.

b. new sneakers and a matching hoodie.

c. a guide dog you could train.

d. a game to play with friends.

e. tickets to a Broadway show.

f. a telescope.

6. Hand me a camera, and I'll . . .

a. zoom in on the petals of a flower.

b. capture my best friend mid-jump.

c. shoot two rocks that look like a heart.

d. squeeze lots of friends into a group selfie.

e. wait for the most colorful sunset.

f. catch a raindrop splash in a puddle.

7. You have to write a book report. You choose a biography about . . .

a. a woman who won a Nobel Prize.

b. a girl who won an Olympic gold medal.

c. the nurse who founded the Red Cross.

d. a woman who was president or prime minister of her country.

e. an Academy Award–winning actress.

f. a famous woman inventor.

Answers

Honor Roll

If you answered **mostly a's**, you're smart stuff. Studying and acing tests are how you shine. Thanks to your hard work and natural curiosity, your hand is the first to shoot up when a teacher asks a tricky question. There's so much to discover about the world around you, and you want to know it all.

truly me Turn to "Super-Cute School Supplies" on page 29 to study in style.

Top Student Athlete

If you answered **mostly b's**, you're A+ in anything active. Gym class, recess, and after-school sports are the highlights of your day. You're full of energy and feel focused when your body is in motion. A run around the track is the perfect prep for sitting still in class or calming nerves before a big test.

truly me Turn to "Spirit Fingers" on page 19 for a craft to cheer on your school team.

MVP
(Most Valuable Pupil)

If you answered **mostly c's,** you're a huge help. If a student needs a tutor, a teacher needs a note taken to the office, or a principal needs a volunteer for the bake sale, you're the first to step forward. You finish your work immediately so that there is plenty of time to lend a hand. Helping others is a good way to learn new skills and share what you know.

truly me Turn to "Study Smarts" on page 33 for a quiz that will help you prepare for a test.

Class President

If you answered **mostly d's,** you're a natural leader. When decisions need to be made, others look to you for a choice that takes everyone into consideration. You're comfortable in front of a group, but you know that it's more about listening to others. You easily set good examples for others through your courage, dependability, and positive attitude.

truly me Turn to "What's in Store?" on page 36 to put your leadership skills to work.

Most Talented

If you answered **mostly e's,** you're a born entertainer. You love to find new ways to express yourself through the clothes you wear, the jokes you tell, or the things you create. You're very outgoing but also enjoy your creative alone time. Your artistic talents shine in the classroom as you find fun ways to use your creativity to help you learn.

truly me Turn to "Hallway Hair" on page 21 for styles that are cool for school.

Science Star

If you answered **mostly f's,** you're an explorer. You spend a lot of time thinking about how things work and coming up with inventions that could make everyday tasks easier. Math and science classes are your favorite, and being outside feels like one big, interesting classroom. You often have questions, and because of that, you'll be a learner for life.

truly me Turn to "Pack Personality" on page 30 for a style quiz perfect for explorers.

Study-and-Stay Sleepover

for 4

Make it a smart night with class-y friends.

Mix up your homework habits! You and three friends can have a study session in style. Invite your pals and their study-buddy dolls to make learning a lot of fun.

Decor

Pretty Pencils

Turn decorative pencils into a darling display piece. Attach pencils to two embroidery hoops using adhesive dots. Place the pencil piece on your table or hang it on the wall. When the party is done, invite your pals to take some pencils home.

Brilliant Banner

Turn mini clipboards (available at office supply stores) into a sign and study surface in one. To each board, clip a decorative piece of paper and one letter to spell out "Be Smart." Once studying is in session, let your friends use the clipboards as on-the-go writing surfaces.

13

Favors

Favors That Rule!
Let your friends know they're the best with a wrapped ruler party favor. Wrap a ruler using the You Rule! punch-out piece in the back of the book. Use tape to secure.

You Rule!

All Write!

All Write!

Turn empty toilet paper rolls into pencil party favors for your friends. Punch out the "pencil tip" circles and fold and cut along the lines provided. Place on the end of a toilet paper roll and tape down. Fill the roll with silly erasers, good-luck notes, and wrapped candies. To make the eraser, cover the other end with pink tissue paper and tape down the edges. Cover the rest of the roll with decorative paper, using double-stick tape to secure the edges. Wrap thin silver duct tape around the eraser's edge. Hand out each to a friend to tell them they're "All Write!"

Well, orange you smart!

Food

Alphabet Study Snack
In a large bowl, combine alphabet-shaped cereal with a couple of other favorite cereals. Add in mini marshmallows, white chocolate chips, nuts, and dried fruit. Mix together and serve with a scoop.

Fun with Fruit
Fold "Well, orange you smart!" flags around mini wooden craft sticks and secure with double-stick tape. With help from a parent, push the sticks into oranges and place in a pretty bowl.

Mini PB&Js
Use cookie cutters to turn a lunch-sack favorite into party appetizers.

This Moo's for You
Serve white and chocolate milk in decorative glass bottles with colorful straws.

Cute Cases

1. Take a piece of felt and cover one side with strips of decorative duct tape so that the top and bottom strips fold over the upper and lower edges of the felt. Make sure that the layers of tape overlap. Trim off any excess tape from the side edges.

2. Fold up the bottom edge of the felt to create a pocket. Use an adhesive dot on each side to help hold in place.

3. Tear off or cut a piece of duct tape so that it's just a little longer than the length from the fold edge to the top. Cover one side of the case with half the width of the tape. Then fold the remaining tape around to the other side. Trim off the top and bottom edges, leaving enough of the ends to stick together. Repeat on the other side.

4. Tear off or cut a 3-inch-long piece of duct tape. Fold it in half like a hot dog bun so that the sticky sides come together. Fold it to make a loop, and attach the ends together with an adhesive dot. Attach the loop to the middle of the case's flap with another adhesive dot.

5. String an extra-long piece of ribbon or cord through the loop. To close, wrap the ends around the bag and tie.

Study Break Smart-Stuff Cuffs

To make a bracelet with adorable designs, apply fabric paint directly to a piece of wax paper. When creating your design, be sure it has a loop of some kind on each side. Let dry overnight; then carefully peel from the wax paper. Cut two pieces of baker's twine so that each is long enough to tie around your wrist. Attach the baker's twine pieces to the loops on the sides and then tie the bracelet around your wrist.

Games

Snowball Pass

Using scraps of old paper, write down one question on each piece. To play, crumple up the pieces of paper and put them in the center of the group. The first person grabs a paper ball and tosses it to another player. That player opens it and then has to answer the question. If she can answer it, she keeps the ball and gets a point. If she can't, she returns it to the pile and chooses another ball to pass to another player. When there are no more paper balls left in the center, the person with the most points wins. Play multiple rounds so that everyone gets a chance to answer different questions.

Speedy Speller

Use the punch-out letters in the back of the book to see if you have a way with words. Using a spelling list, have one person be the reader and timekeeper. On Go, start the clock and see how quickly the player can spell all the words on the list. Each player gets a turn. The person with the fastest time wins. Play a similar game when you need to learn vocabulary words. The reader says the definition, and the player has to spell the word.

Spirit Fingers

Show off your school spirit by attaching premade pom-poms (available at craft stores) in your team colors to the fingertips of knit gloves.

Using a plastic needle and a 12-inch length of yarn, string one end of the yarn through the middle of one pom-pom and then through the tip of one glove finger. Remove the needle and tie the ends of the yarn in a knot so that it is hidden beneath the pom-pom. Snip off the ends and complete for each finger of the glove. Tie two extra pom-poms to your doll's hands so that she can be your fellow fan.

Subject Style

Decorate your notebooks with oodles of doodles.

Instead of hiding your doodles in the margins, share them for all students to see. Punch out the notebook labels and decorate them with markers using colors you love. When you're done, use double-stick tape to attach the labels to your notebooks' front covers. You'll be organized and stylish!

Hallway Hair

Try these super styles to be head of the class.

Some people think school means fitting in, and while that's sometimes true, it doesn't mean you have to go unnoticed. You're special and should let that shine. Give these hairstyles a try, and see which ones make you feel unique.

1. Starting behind one ear, part your hair over the top of your head to make a ponytail. (Pick up about half of your hair.) Secure with an elastic, pulling the hair partway through the last time to make a loop.

2. Use the back hair to make another ponytail slightly to the side of the first one. Secure with an elastic.

3. Adjust loops. Wrap a few strands of hair around the loops to cover the elastics, and secure with hairpins or tiny clips.

21

Twin Twists

1. Separate a section of hair at the top of the head near the face. Twist hair tightly and secure on the side of the head with a clip.

2. Separate another section of hair below the first section. Twist hair tightly.

3. Combine the second twist with the ends of the first twist and secure with a clip. Gently comb out loose ends of twists.

1. Gather hair near the face into one small section on each side. Braid each section and secure with hair elastics.

2. Gather the braids together and twist to the end while slowly pulling up, making a roll.

3. Coil the roll around itself to make a bun. Insert hairpins to hold in place.

Braid Bun

Friendship Frame Garland

Frame your friends' school photos and hang them as a garland in your locker or at home.

To make garland:

1. Carefully punch out the frames from the back of this book and pop out the center of each one.

2. Glue the top of each frame to a ribbon (found at craft stores) and let dry. Leave an inch between frames.

3. Add your friends' photos to the garland!

A Bit About Me

Fill in the blanks to create a keepsake of yourself as a student.

I'm pretty awesome at
_____
_____
_____
_____

My teacher is
_____
_____
_____
_____

If I were principal, I would
_____
_____
_____
_____

I love hanging out with
_____
_____
_____

My school mascot looks like this:

Top 3 Best School Subjects:
_____
_____
_____

Today,_____,
fill in date
I want a career as a
_____
_____
_____

The Grossest School Lunch Award goes to

_____
_____
_____
_____

The perfect place to go on a field trip is

_____
_____
_____

The funniest thing that has happened at school is

_____
_____
_____
_____

My School Schedule:

_____
_____
_____
_____
_____

5 Things I Must Do This Year:

1. _____
2. _____
3. _____
4. _____
5. _____

Dream Subject to Study:

_____
_____
_____

This summer will be all about

_____
_____
_____
_____

After school, I

_____
_____
_____

IT'S **AWESOME TODAY**

Super-Cute School Supplies

Accessorize your school tools with these perfect punch-outs.

Don't forget:

This book belongs to
....

Study for:

Write On

Super Student

I've got this!

Smarty Pants

Pack Personality

See what tote is totally right for you!

⭐ Start here!

What does your lunch look like?

Paper bag

radio.

You usually listen to music from a

playlist/ MP3/ phone.

Cute lunch box or tote

boutiques and vintage shops.

You like to shop at

Cafeteria tray

the mall.

Your locker most likely has

sticky notes, a calendar, a mirror.

Easy to manage—ponytail/braid/headband

wallpaper, friend pics, and posters.

Which hairstyle is more you?

Standout—more stylish; looks like time and effort are required

New girl

You get to pick your lab partner for the day. Whom do you choose?

BFF

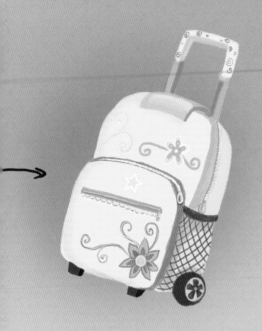

Rolling Bag

You're Miss Practical. You're all about working smarter, not harder, which is why the rolling tote is the best bag for you. You might stand out a bit from other students, but that's cool, because you're staying true to who you are. Roll on!

Messenger Bag/ Stylish Tote

Your trendsetting ways make a stylish tote the cutest carryall for you. You're a style trailblazer and you like to shake things up with what you wear. Every new look isn't always right for you, but it takes courage just to try. Stay chic!

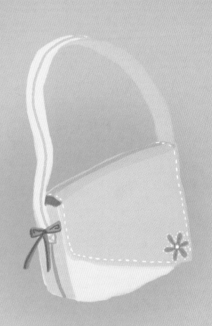

Backpack

You're all about blending in, and for that, the backpack can't be beat. You're perfectly OK with being part of the crowd, so long as it means all eyes are not on you. You're most comfortable with your close friends, and they love you for being you.

Study Smarts

1. When you get stuck on a homework problem, the first thing you do is . . .
a. review your textbook and notes.
b. take a break from it and work on something else for a while.
c. plan to ask the teacher about it in the morning.

2. When studying for a test, you . . .
a. tackle the hard stuff first so that you have enough time to focus on it.
b. skim your notes and jot down things you need to work on.
c. work on the easy things first and fit in whatever hard stuff you can before your favorite show starts.

3. Where is the best study spot?
a. Sitting at my desk
b. Lounging on my bed
c. Wherever

4. What is the best time of day to study?
a. Right after school
b. Before bed
c. In the morning before school

5. You tend to study best when . . .
a. there is complete silence.
b. there is some noise, but not too much or too little.
c. there is a lot going on around you.

6. You prefer to work . . .
a. until everything is finished.
b. with breaks for texting a friend and eating snacks.
c. in quick bursts, so as not to get bored.

7. When you have to work in groups, you . . .
a. groan. You'd rather just do it yourself.
b. hope that you get to work with at least one of your friends.
c. know this is going to be the best time to share your new joke.

8. If you were in a study group, you'd most likely . . .
a. make a to-do list so that everyone stays on track.
b. bring a game to get everyone's brains going.
c. supply the candy to bribe someone to help you.

33

Answers

Bright Bulb

If you chose **mostly a's,** you're a true bookworm. Your goal is to get good grades, and that means homework and study time come first. You prefer to finish projects before they're due so that you never have to cram before class. Teachers can count on you with the answers, and your friends call you when they're stuck and can't solve a problem. You're at the head of the class, but don't forget that you need to have a little fun, too. That doesn't mean you should slack off and let your grades slide, but reward yourself for a job well done.

Study Tips

Treat yourself to something fun whenever you reach a goal. Give yourself a manicure. Take your dog for a walk. Or chat with your friend on the phone.

Try some yoga poses before you dive right into your assignments. Loosening up the body and taking some belly breaths will help you to relax a bit.

Look for a study buddy who has a style similar to yours. Pair up with her to prepare for a test and see how you can help each other shine even brighter.

Classroom Casual

If you chose **mostly b's,** you're a well-balanced student. You're serious about school, but not so much that it's going to stress you out. Studying with friends, drawing a colorful cover for a book report, and using clever rhymes to remember things are all creative ways you make school more fun. Your casual style will keep you passing with flying colors, but don't get too comfy. Some assignments are going to need your full attention, so look for ways to get focused and sharp when you need to.

Study Tips

Decorate your desk so that it feels like your perfect place to study.

Join a study group and see what tips you can learn from others.

Pick project and essay topics that are different for you. If you usually go for creative topics, try something that's historical or science-related.

A Bit Too Laid-Back

If you chose **mostly c's,** studying and homework aren't at the top of your list. You prefer playing instead of working on projects, and TV time instead of study time. Your classmates like that you're silly, but your teacher would rather you be more serious. Even if you're getting good grades now, classes may get more challenging as you get older. It's best to find a study style that works for you now so that you don't run the risk of falling behind later.

Study Tips

Ask a dedicated student if she'd be willing to share her study secrets with you.

Find ways to turn homework or studying into a game, using a timer, song lyrics, and game board pieces to help you.

Get some exercise. Sitting in class can make you antsy. Set aside some time to burn off your extra energy before study time starts.

What's in Store?

Lend your school a helping hand by selling supplies to students.

Pens 50¢

Pencils 40¢

Sticky Notes 10¢

Pencils 40¢

Markers 25¢

Pencils 40¢

School Store

Who's in Charge?

Since you can't just start selling items from your backpack, the first thing to do is get the OK from your school administration. Ask your teacher for advice on who would make this decision. If she doesn't know, check with the principal's office.

Make a Plan

Once you know who makes the big decisions, don't just rush into her office and ask for an answer. Starting a school store is a big job and one that will cost the school money to start. You'll need to prove that you and whoever else will be running the store are responsible students and have the time to take on the task. You'll also need to have a good reason for starting a store. Here are some examples:

- You would like to raise money for a school need, such as new art supplies, new basketball uniforms, or extra computers.

- You hope to earn funds for something fun: class field trips, an after-school club, or a school pizza party.

- You and your classmates want to give back to the community or to a charity. Maybe the local library needs new books. Or maybe a school in another state was affected by a natural disaster. The money from the school store can be donated to help.

Set the Specifics

If the school store gets approved, you'll also need to figure out the following:

Hours
What time will the store be open? When is it easiest for students to run the store and shop at the store?

Location
Can a table be set up in the hallway? Can a supply closet serve double duty? Is space available in the cafeteria?

Security
Where will the profits and merchandise be safe when the store isn't open? Who will have access?

Helping Hands

Since you won't be able to run the school store all by yourself, round up other students interested in helping out. You could even consider asking your math teacher if she'd take it on as a class project. Students would learn a lot about money and math skills, and everyone could participate toward making the store a success.

Ask Permission

You're now ready to ask for permission. Schedule a time to meet with the person in charge, explaining what it is you'd like to talk about. During your meeting time, be polite and explain all of the details you've worked out.

If the Answer Is No . . .

Bummer! But at least you tried. There might be lots of reasons not to open a school store: Maybe there was one in the past and students weren't interested, maybe there was no space to store supplies, or maybe it interfered too much with class time. Whatever the reason, come up with other ways to raise money. Be creative, or give one of these a ideas a try:

Craft Sale

Bake Sale

Car Wash

Fun Fair

Movie Night

Raffle Tickets

If the Answer Is Yes . . .

Congrats! It's time to get to work.

What to Sell?

Students use lots of items in school every day, so start with those. Things like folders, paper, pens, erasers, and rulers are all good choices. But don't forget to include fun items, too. Work with the teacher or administrator to see if your budget will allow . . .

locker posters.

items with the school logo and mascot—clothing, tote bags, locker clings.

things kids can wear—bracelets and hair ties.

snacks—granola bars and candy, if they're allowed in school.

school spirit items—foam fingers, megaphones, pom-poms.

Make Dazzling Displays

Customers will buy only if they know what you are selling. If you have a small space, put out only one or two pieces of each item, and keep the rest in boxes or containers that you can easily pull from. If space allows, try to show off your merchandise in ways that attract the eye. Make signs with prices, and even use your doll to display that day's deals. Don't forget to work with a teacher to price the items you're going to sell!

Customers First

It's important to be nice to all the customers who come to the store, and do your best to answer their questions. Never ignore your shoppers.

Spread the Word

If business is slow, be sure students know about the store. Ask to have the store hours read during announcements. Also, get permission to put up posters and flyers to announce the grand opening. If nothing else, have your friends help you spread the word.

A school store is fun to run and can be the perfect way to raise money, but it's a big responsibility, too. If you're not quite ready to be a business owner, play pretend school store with your doll at home. Use supplies you already have to create a chic school-supply boutique in your own room!

Here are some other American Girl books you might like:

Doll School

Doll Art Studio

Doll Tees Felt Fashions

Doll Dining

Doll at Work

play@
☆American Girl™

Discover online games, quizzes, activities,
and more at **americangirl.com/play**

You Rule!

You Rule!

You Rule!

You Rule!

Pencil Tips

Pencil Wrapper

All Write!

All Write!

Pencil Tips

Pencil Wrapper

All Write!

All Write!

Well,
orange
you smart!

Well,
orange
you smart!

Well,
orange
you smart!

Well,
orange
you smart!

A A A A A A B
B C C D D D E
E E E E E F F
G G H H H I I
I I I I J J K
K L L L M M M
N N N N O O O
O O P P Q Q R
R R R R S S S
S S T T T T T
U U U U U V V W
W X X Y Y Z Z

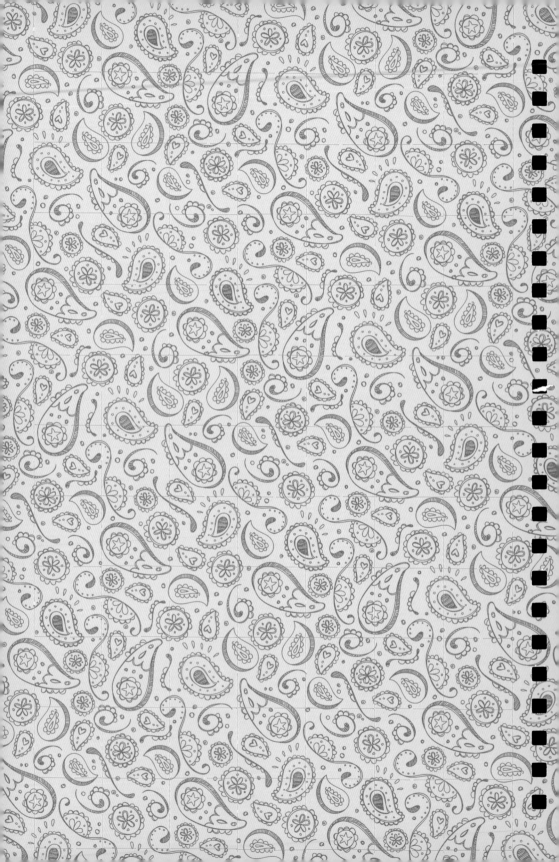